Within.

OR

The Kingdom of God is Within You.

BY

Rev. Andrew Murray.

Within. Copyright 1897 Andrew Murray.
This work is in the Public Domain

Note

The first three Addresses contained in this volume were delivered at the Mowbray Convention, Cape of Good Hope, and have since been revised and corrected by the Author.

Within.

Table of Contents.

The Kingdom of God......................7
The Indwelling of God.................22
Jesus Christ in You......................35
Daily Fellowship with God...........51

1

The Kingdom of God.

THE FIRST MEETING of a Convention in a new place is often a difficult one. The most of us are strangers to each other. An atmosphere of prayer and love has hardly yet been created. We do not know whether all understand the object of our meeting. But I am sure we may look to our Father in heaven to melt our hearts into one. We can ask Him by His Holy Spirit to make us of one heart and one mind in seeking His glory, in trusting His mighty power, and in looking to Him alone for a blessing. Let us all from the very commencement of our Convention look to God, not only for what each one needs for himself, but as members of one body, with the fervent prayer that there may be a blessing for all. Let us unite ourselves before God as a company of His own dear children, full of love to each other, and with the confident assurance that He will bless us. Our Father, do

Thou melt our hearts into one by Thy Holy Spirit. Thou knowest the need of each one; let Thy word meet it. Give Thy servants grace so to speak that Thy children may know what their God has for them, and what they may expect Him to do for them.

The words from which I wish to speak tonight you will find in Mark 10:15, "Verily I say unto you, whosoever shall not receive the Kingdom of God as a little child, he shall not enter therein."

Listen again: *"Verily I say unto you, whosoever shall not receive the Kingdom of God as a little child, he shall not enter therein."* We need at the opening of our Convention to look forward to all that we are going to speak and to hear during the coming days, and to try and take our right place before God. I think this word of the Lord Jesus will guide us exactly to where we ought to be. It will tell us what God asks of us if we are even now to enter His Kingdom and live in it: that each of us receive it into our hearts as a little child. These are the two things we need to know, to enter into the enjoyment of a full salvation. With these two things all our Convention teaching will be occupied: the wonderful blessing God has for us, the wonderful way in which we are to become possessors of it.

Four simple expressions.

My text has four simple expressions that we need to understand if we are to enter into its meaning and power. We must ask: 1. What is *the Kingdom of God?* 2. What is it to *enter the Kingdom?* 3. What to *receive the Kingdom?* 4. What to receive the Kingdom *as a little child?*

First: What is the Kingdom of God? You know how both John the Baptist preached that the Kingdom of God or of heaven had come nigh. During the Old Testament times it had been spoken of, and promised, and hoped for, but it had not come. During the life of Christ on earth there were mighty tokens of its coming and its nearness, but it had not yet come in power. What it would be Christ foretold when He once said, "the Kingdom of God is within you;" and another time, "There be some standing here who shall not see death, till they see the Kingdom of God come in power." On the day of Pentecost that word was fulfilled. The Holy Spirit brought down out of heaven the Kingdom of God into the hearts of the disciples, and they went forth and preached the Gospel of the Kingdom not as at hand or coming, but as come.

The Kingdom of God.

It is not difficult now to answer the question what is ***the Kingdom of God?*** It is that spiritual state in which the life of God and of heaven is made accessible to men, and they enter into its enjoyment here on earth. If we ask what its marks are we find the answer in the wondrous change we see in the life of the disciples.

The mark of a kingdom is the presence of the king. With the Holy Spirit Christ came down to be with His disciples as really, and more nearly, than when He was with them in the flesh. The abiding nearness and fellowship of Christ, and in Him of God the Father, is the very central blessing of the Kingdom. This experience was what the Holy Spirit at Pentecost made real. The disciples had their Lord with them as consciously as the angels in heaven. His Presence made heaven all around and in them. A believer to whom a full entrance into the Kingdom is given, has the Presence of God and Christ as the good part that cannot be taken away.

The mark of a kingdom is the rule of the king. We read, "His Kingdom ruleth over all." Before Pentecost the disciples could not love or be humble, could not trust or be bold. But when the kingdom came the dominion of God prevailed, God's Presence through the Holy Spirit gained the victory, sin was overcome, and the will of God done in them as in heaven. When Jesus taught them to pray, "Thy Kingdom come, Thy will be done on earth as in heaven," He promised this. As the Kingdom came down with the Holy Ghost the promise was fulfilled. And our entering into the kingdom means our being brought into a life in which God rules over all, His will is truly and joyfully done, and all the blessedness that reigns in heaven finds its counterpart here below. As it is written, "The Kingdom of God is righteousness, and peace, and joy in the Holy Ghost."

The mark of a kingdom is power. "The Kingdom of God is not in word but in power." Just think of the work these simple fishermen dared to undertake, and were able to accomplish. Think of the weapon with which they had to do their work—the despised Gospel of the crucified Nazarene. Think of all that God wrought through them, and see how the coming of the Kingdom brought a new power from heaven by which feeble men were made mighty through God, and the slaves of Satan were made God's holy children.

Believers! it is this Kingdom of God come from heaven we preach. We come to tell you that a life in the presence and the will and the power of God, has been opened up, that men have been brought to enter into it and live in it, and that you too can enter in. There are some of you who are confessing the feebleness of your Christian life, and the failure of all your efforts to make it better. You have believed in Jesus as your Saviour, but of an entrance into the Kingdom as it came in power you know nothing. I beseech you begin at once tonight and believe that there is such a life in the kingdom here on earth. Believe that Christ's death wrought such a wonderful and complete redemption, and that the coming down of the Holy Spirit, nothing else but the glorified Christ coming in the Spirit, brought down the heavenly life in such reality, that, even as the first disciples, we can be endued with power from on high. If you will believe that, if you will hold fast, there is a kingdom of heaven on earth, your desire will be stirred to become partakers of its blessedness, and as we point out the way how, your hope will begin to see that this life is even for you too. And you will be prepared to accept all that Jesus has to teach us in His word.

Enter the Kingdom.

This is our second question. What is it to **enter the Kingdom?** You know the meaning of the word enter. It is most commonly used in Scripture of the entrance of the children of Israel into the land of promise, and of the believer's entrance by faith into the rest of God.

Entrance: The word simply means coming into full possession or enjoyment. And it is just this Christ means and you long for with regard to the Kingdom, when He speaks here of entering it. The word does not refer to heaven, and our entering that when we die. It speaks of the kingdom of heaven come to earth, and our entering into it in power, as the disciples did at Pentecost. There are many Christians who are content with a heaven after death. The promise of living in a kingdom of heaven here on earth has no attraction, and wakens no response. They cannot understand what we mean. But there are hearts in whom the longing has been wakened for something better, and who would fain know what it is to enter the Kingdom.

Entrance means coming into full possession. Just think of the blessings of the Kingdom we mentioned. God's manifested presence with us without ceasing; God's blessed rule and dominion over us established, so that His heavenly will is done in us and by us; God's mighty power descending upon us, so that through us Christ can do His work of saving souls. Into a life in which these blessings are your daily experience, you can enter even now. That life has been prepared for you, and is promised; it is waiting for you. You can enter even now by faith. As an army conquers and enters a city, so many a one struggles and fights and seeks to take the Kingdom by violence. And he fails. We can only enter by faith. As Joshua brought Israel into the land of promise, and Jericho fell without a blow being struck, our Lord Jesus waits to bring us into the good land. It was He who from heaven gave the disciples their abundant entrance into the Kingdom; it is He who still by His Holy Spirit will lead each one of us in. By faith in Him He brings us in.

Receive the Kingdom.

You want to know what this faith is, and how it is to act. Listen to what our Lord tells us. Our third question was what is it to ***receive the Kingdom?*** What is the difference between the two expressions our Lord uses: entering the Kingdom and receiving the Kingdom? You see He makes the latter, receiving, the condition of the former, entering in. The one is active: I enter in and take possession. The other is passive: I receive. The words give expression to the great truth that before I can enter the Kingdom, it must first enter into me. Before I can possess its privileges and powers, it must first possess me, with all my powers and being. I must, in subjection and surrender, in poverty and emptiness, receive the Kingdom into my heart before *I* am fit to be entrusted with all the power and glory it offers me. What is dark and evil within must first be cast out; what is of God must fill my being; that which is born of God alone, can inherit the Kingdom and its heavenly life. There must be a heavenly nature before there can be a heavenly state.

Receive the Kingdom: the word is very simple. It implies two things: there is one who gives, and another who accepts. How many there are who have heard of the blessed life in the Kingdom, and the wonderful joy it gives, and who have never thought that it must be received from the living God Himself. What we need is to be brought to such consciousness of our utter ignorance and impotence, that we feel we cannot grasp or apprehend this wonderful salvation that is offered, but that we are to come into contact with the Father in heaven, and as a heavenly bestowal, receive from Him the Kingdom in power. And that not as something that we have to persuade Him to give us, but as the child's portion that actually belongs to us, and that He yearns to see us enjoy. It is as we believe this, and look up to the everlasting God, infinitely ready and able to give the Kingdom in its power into our very heart, that our hearts will take courage to expect that the Kingdom with its blessings can, indeed, enter into us.

Then our accepting will become so simple. When we see the God who has promised, in His infinite love, just as the sun seeks to enter with its light and life into every little flower and every blade of grass, longing to enter into us, and be all that as God He can be, we shall understand how our place is simply to rest in what He will do, to claim His great gift of the Spirit who brings the Kingdom into us, and to wait in patient dependence for Him to do His mighty work. Our position day by day will be as of those who, having accepted, now count upon God to reveal and work in us all that he has for us.

You may be inclined to ask, If the receiving be so simple, how is it that it still is so difficult, and that so few really find what they seek? The answer is, the whole thing is so simple, but we are not simple. The simplicity of the thing is its difficulty, because we have lost our simplicity. It is this Jesus teaches us in the words He adds, and which we must still speak of.

As a little child.

What is it to receive the Kingdom ***as a little child?*** Have we any illustration of this in nature? Yes. How did the Prince of Wales become heir to the throne of England? By his birth as a little child he received the kingdom. He was born to it. And so we must be born by the Holy Spirit into that disposition of heart or childlike simplicity which will receive the Kingdom as a little child. When a little child receives a kingdom, it does so as a feeble, helpless little thing. As it grows up and hears of what is coming to it, it does so in simple trustfulness and gladness. Even so Jesus calls us to become little children and as such to receive the Kingdom.

Oh! how hard it is for men and women, with their will and their strength and their wisdom, with all the power of self and the old man, to become as little children. It is impossible. And yet without this we cannot enter the Kingdom and its heavenly life. We can know about the

Kingdom, we may taste some of its powers, we may work for it and often rejoice in it—but we cannot enter in fully and entirely, until we become as a little child. And with men this is impossible. But with God all things are possible.

There are some things we can do towards it. We can yield to the teaching of God's Spirit when He convinces us of our pride and self-confidence. We can confess our self-will and self-effort. We can pray and long and strive after the childlike spirit. We can go as far as Peter and the disciples did before Pentecost. But the little-child nature that enters into the Kingdom, the Holy Spirit, the Spirit of God's Son, who cries Abba, Father, the Spirit that claims and expects and receives all from God alone, alone can give. He is within you, as the Spirit of Christ, to work this: He gives the grace to become a little child, and so He fits the heart for receiving from heaven His fullness, as He brings the Kingdom in heavenly power.

How to become a little child? How to lose all our strength and wisdom, our will and life, and be as little newborn children? Oh that I knew the way hither, you cry. Look to Jesus! As a babe in Bethlehem, He was born heir to the Kingdom of David. He grew up to manhood, and then giving up His will in Gethsemane when he cried Abba, Father, He gave up His life, and was laid in the dark grave in the helplessness of death. Thence he arose, as the firstbegotten of the dead, born again out of the dead to the Throne of Glory. In the feebleness of the grave He gained His throne. We need to die with Christ—that is the way to get delivered from the old man and self, the way to receive the heavenly life as a little child, and so to enter the Kingdom. The feebleness of Bethlehem and the manger, of Calvary and the grave, was Christ's way to enter the Kingdom—for us there is no other way.

As we seek to humble ourselves and renounce all wish and all hope of being or doing good of ourselves, as we yield all our human ability and energy to the death in the confession that it is nothing but sinful and worthy of death, God's Spirit will make the power of Christ's death to sin work in us, we shall die with Him, and with Him be raised in newness of life. And the new life will be the little child that receives the Kingdom.

Two simple truths.

The four thoughts Christ's words have suggested indicate some of the truths that will occupy us during the coming days of the Convention. We are going tomorrow to speak of the needs of the Church, and next day of what God is willing to do for His people. The speakers will probably tell us how little we see the Kingdom of God come in power among God's children. Let us begin this evening by each of us asking himself—How is it with me? Am I proving, in my own experience and to others, that it has come, and that a child of God can enter in and live in all the blessedness of its heavenly life? Have I by the Holy Spirit so received the Kingdom into my heart, that the presence and power of God manifested in me, and Himself working out His will in me and through me, are indeed the strength and joy of my religion? Let nothing less than the possession of this satisfy us, let this be our one desire with this Convention.

To this end let us hold fast two things. The one, the unspeakable blessedness, the divine possibility, the absolute certainty of the Kingdom of God in power being the portion of God's people. Our heart is meant to be the very dwelling of God living in it. The Holy Spirit is meant so to be in us and through us that all the action of the heart, all that is done by it, is to be done by the Holy Spirit inspiring it. The Kingdom of Heaven has come to earth and can be set up within us in such power, that the presence and the will and the power of God shall be our life and joy. It is more than the mind can grasp: let us believe it. Our wonder-working God will make it true.

The other thing is this. Let us believe that all that is needed to be in full possession of these blessings is what the Holy Spirit, who is already in us, will work. He will make us as little children before God. He will enable us as such to receive the Kingdom from the Father, He will lead us and bring us in, so that we enter into the Kingdom and the heavenly life it gives.

Shall we not tonight at once say: Lord! nothing less than this can satisfy me. I want to live my life fully in thy kingdom. I yield myself, I yield self with all its life to thee. In the faith of the Holy Spirit I say: Here I am as a little child; Father, in the gift of Thy Spirit in Pentecostal power, let me receive the Kingdom as a little child.

2

The Indwelling of God.

What agreement hath the temple of God with idols? for ye are the temple of the living God; as God hath said, I will dwell in them and walk in them; and I will be their God, and they shall be my people. —II Corinthians 6:16.

WE HAVE HERE an answer to the question, How is God going to be my God? Am I to regard Him as a great and Almighty and distant God, outside of me and separate from me in the heaven above, from whom I am from time to time to have a little help? That is what many Christians think, and it is owing to, this thought of God that they experience so little of His real presence and power. No, this thought of God is only the beginning of true faith in Him. As we learn to know Scripture better, and the deep need of our heart, and the wonderful love of God that longs to enter completely into us, we learn that there is something better. The question, *How is*

God going to be my God? finds its answer in the words I have just read. *"God hath said, I will dwell in them, and I will be their God"* That is God's answer to your question.

And what a wonderful answer it is. You know what a difference there is between the things that surround us and force themselves on our notice and occupy us, but which we never give a place in our heart, and others that enter into us and take possession of our very life. A mother has a place for a child in her heart—it lives there. The gold of a miser has his heart, with all its love and hope. How little we think that our heart was actually created that God might dwell there, that He might show forth His life and love there, and that there our love and joy might be in Him alone. How little we know that just as naturally as we have the love of parents or children filling our heart and making us happy, we can have the living God, for whom the heart was made, dwelling there and filling it with His own goodness and blessedness. This is my message this evening: God wants your heart; if you give it Him, He will dwell in it.

You heard what was said this afternoon about God, and what He was to the Psalmist, in Psalm 42 and 43, as he calls Him, "the end of my life, the God of my strength, end of my exceeding joy, and my end." But how is God to be the strength of my life and my God? In no other way but by coming into my life with His Divine life, and so filling it with His Almighty strength—then He is the strength of my life. With His holy life and love He comes into my heart, the very seat and centre of my life, and acts within me as my God, working out my life for me. He makes divinely and blessedly true what is written here: "God hath said, I will dwell in them, and so I will be their God."

Do you not think it would make a wonderful difference in our life if we really believed this, and in believing received the blessing it speaks of? What a holy awe there would be in us. And what a tender fear lest we should hurt or grieve this holy, loving God. What a longing would be awakened—I want to know how to walk with this God and have full communion with Him. And what a bright confidence: now my God has come to dwell in me, I need fear no more that I shall not have His presence, or that He will not do for me and in me all I need.

I want to speak to you very simply about this wonderful indwelling, and to give a few thoughts that may help you to see how it is the very essence of true Christianity—the very thing man as a sinner needed to have restored to him, and the very thing Christ Jesus came to give.

And let me say in the first place, that it was for nothing less, and nothing else, than *this indwelling that man was created by God.* Have you ever wondered why God created man at all? The reason was this. God brought creatures into existence that He might show forth and impart His own divine goodness and glory to them in a creaturely fashion, so that they, as far as they were capable of it, might share with Him His divine perfections and blessedness. And He specially created man in His own image and likeness, that in him He might show how the Life of God could dwell in the human creature, and gradually fit him and lift him up for dwelling with God and in God through eternity. God's love said: in his measure, I want man to be as holy and as good and as blessed as I am. I cannot give him the holiness or blessedness apart from Myself, but I can and will dwell in him, in the inmost depths of his life, and be to him his goodness and his strength. Yes, this was the glory of the divine creating love—God wanted to give man all He had Himself—God gave Himself to be his life and joy.

In no other possible way could God do this

but by dwelling in him. Just as an oil lamp has its light inside, and through the globe gives light all around, so the God of love created man that He might be within him the light of his life. This was to be man's dignity and his blessedness, that in and through him all the glories of the blessed God should ever be shining out before the universe. Our whole nature, will and affections, and powers, were all to be the vessel to receive and hold and overflow with the blessed fullness of the life of God in us. And it was to be man's high prerogative and privilege just to offer and yield himself to God in the consciousness of this holy partnership. What God was in himself in heaven, living out His own life there, that He was to be on earth in and through man, living out His own life as truly as in heaven. Oh! the glory and the bliss of being a man! Glory to God for our creation.

But now, look next in the light of this blessed truth, *I will dwell in them,* at what sin has done. God had made man to be His home, His temple, where His presence, His will would be all in all. It is of this indwelling that sin has robbed both God and us. The temptation with which Satan came to man in Paradise really meant this—would he with his whole heart yield to God as Father and Master, giving him

His place and doing His will alone? Or would he not do his own will, and let self rule as master in his own house? Alas! that fatal choice. God was dethroned and cast out of His temple, and self set upon the throne. Just as really as in later days the image of an idol was set up in the very home that God had caused to be built for us Himself, so self was enthroned in the seat of God. The description of the man of sin, when he is fully revealed come to full maturity, "who opposeth and exalteth himself above all that is called God, or that is worshipped, so that he as God sitteth in the temple of God and showeth himself that he is God," is the true self at every stage and in every state: self sits in the temple of God as God. All the sin of heathendom—and how awful it is—and all the sin of Christendom—no less terrible!—is but the outgrowth of that one root—God dethroned, self-enthroned, in the heart of man. All the sin and sorrow of the life of each one of us has been nothing but this: you were not what you were created to be—you had not God dwelling in your heart to fill it with His life and peace and love. I can with confidence ask any man here, Would you be content to have all filthy reptiles and animals occupy your houses along with yourselves? Would you allow other people to be masters in the home you dwell in? You never would. And yet, alas! you allow so much else to occupy the heart and have the place God alone is meant to have. And so many are quite unconscious of it. We come tonight with the message: let there be an end of all this desecration of God's temple. God asks your whole heart for Himself—oh! let it be given to Him.

    A third thought is, in the light of this indwelling of God, look at *Christ's work of redemption.* What was the object of Christ's coming from Heaven? It was to show us the possibility and the blessedness of being a man with God living His life in Him. We teach children by means of pictures and models. When God's Son became man, He lived a perfect human life—"made like us in all things"—and told us it was by the power of the Father dwelling in Him. "I do nothing of Myself—the Father in Me doeth the work." Here is no question of abstract thought or deep theology—here is a true man, sleeping, hungering, wearied, tempted, weeping, suffering like ourselves, telling us that the Father dwells in Him, and that this is the secret of His perfect, blessed life. He felt it all just as we feel it, but He could do and bear all because the Father was in Him. He showed us how a man can live, and how He would enable us to live.

When He had done this in His life, He died that He might deliver us from the power of sin, and open up the way for us to return to God. On the cross He proved that a man in whom God dwells will be ready to suffer anything and to give his life even to the death, that he may enter into the fullness of the life of God. When sin entered, man lost the life of God dwelling in him, and became dead to it. There was no way for man to be freed from the life of sin but by dying to it. Christ died to sin, that He might take us up into His fellowship and that we too might be dead to sin, and live unto God with His own life. And so He won back for us the life man had been created for, with God dwelling in him, by giving to us His life, the very life He had lived. As He spake, "As Thou, Father, art in Me, and I in Thee, that they may be one in us."

Oh! my beloved fellow Christians, this is the salvation Christ has won for us: a deliverance from self by a death to it in the death of the cross; a restoration to the life we were created for, with our heart a home for God.

And how now are we to become partakers of this salvation? Look once again in the light of this blessed truth of the divine indwelling at Pentecost and the coming of the Holy Spirit.

Have you realised what the meaning is of God's sending the Holy Spirit into our hearts? It is nothing less than this—Christ who had been with the disciples on earth, but not in them, came back to them in the Spirit, now to dwell in them just as He had before dwelt with them. All that we read of the wondrous change that came over the disciples—their selfishness changed into love, their pride into humility, their fear of suffering into boldness and joy, their unbelief into fullness of faith, their feebleness into power—was owing to this one thing—the glorified Christ had come to dwell within them as their life. That was the joy of Pentecost in heaven: God regained possession of His temple, and could now again dwell in men as He had meant to do before the fall. The temple of which Christ had said that it should be broken down, was the temple of His body, in its connection with our sin laid upon Him. The temple He was to build in three days was His resurrection body, with its holy, heavenly life. In union with it we are now the temple of the living God. The Holy Spirit takes possession in the name of the Three-One God; and the Father and the Son come to make abode with us.

When we look at the great promise—"I will dwell in them"—and its fulfilment at Pentecost, we are reminded of the great difference between the preparatory working of the Spirit in conversion and regeneration, and His Pentecostal indwelling. The former every Christian must have: without that there is no life. The life may be feeble and sickly, still where there is life, it is the Spirit's working. But that is only to prepare the temple. Pentecost is the glory of God filling the temple, God coming to abide. Let us believe that the promise can and will be fulfilled.

One more thought. In the light of our text *look at the state of the Church of Christ.* How many believers there are of whom one would never say that their hearts are a temple that God has cleansed, and where He dwells. How much there is of coldness and worldliness, and selfishness and sin, and inconsistency of profession, that makes one sometimes doubt whether there are Christians at all. The state of Christ's Church is sad indeed. How little zeal for God's honour, delight in His fellowship, devotion to His service and kingdom, how little of a life in the power of the Holy Spirit. It surely manifests that the promise "I will dwell in them" has never been understood, or believed, or claimed by a large majority of Christians.

Let me ask, Have you claimed it? Do you

seek to live it out? If not, the one great object of our Convention is to set before you this blessed life to which God has redeemed you, to urge and to help you to enter upon it and walk in it.

Need I tell you what the way is. Begin by confessing how little you have even sought to live as God's temple. Think of how it must have grieved the love of your Father, that after all he had done through His Son and Spirit to get his abode again, you have cared so little to know about it or seek for it. Confess, too, your helplessness. You have tried to be better than you are, and you have failed. You must fail, until you receive His word that nothing less is needed, nothing less is offered, than that God Himself become the strength of your life.

Set your heart upon the blessing. You know how desire is the great moving power of the world. Fix your desire upon this divine, this wondrous grace: "I will dwell in them." Let no thought of your unworthiness or feebleness discourage you. Here is something that is impossible with man: but with God it is possible. He can and will fulfil His promise. Let it become the one desire of your heart. Understand that this is the salvation the Holy Spirit brings you as soon as you are ready to give up all for it. As soon as the heart is ready to lose all, to be emptied of all, to be cleansed of all that is of self or nature, the promise will surely be fulfilled—"I will dwell in them, and I will be their God."

"Wherefore," hear now the words that follow immediately on my text: "Wherefore come out from among them and be ye separate, saith the Lord, and touch not the unclean thing, and I will receive you." Come out from all that is of the world and a worldly religion, from all that is inconsistent with the holy privilege of being God's holy temple and dwelling. Come out and be separate, take your stand as one who is going to live a life different from the crowd around you, be separate unto God and His will. "And touch not the unclean thing"—be as a cleansed temple where nothing that defiles in the very least may enter—be wholly for God and holy to God—and He will make His word good: "I will dwell in you." He Himself will reveal and impart and maintain within you all that the promise means.

Believer! will you accept of this full salvation? Will you do it now? I pray you, reject not this wonderful love. Oh! let your God have you, to satisfy His love and yours by dwelling in you. This moment accept it, and you can trust Him to work it in you. Amen.

3

Jesus Christ in You.

THE WORDS FROM which I wish to speak to you this evening, will take us back to the subject that we had last night. It is one of such deep importance—*the indwelling of God*—one to which believers are in many cases so unaccustomed, and one which, even when its truth is accepted, cannot be apprehended in its fullness all at once, that it may be well to come back to it again. My text is *II Corinthians 13:5*, "Examine yourselves whether ye be in the faith; prove your own selves. Know ye not your own selves how that *Jesus Christ is in you,* except ye be reprobates?"

Every thoughtful Bible-reader knows that the state of the Corinthian Church was a very sad one. There were terrible sins among them, and both epistles are full of sorrow and reproof. At the close of the second epistle, Paul sums up all his pleadings in this one question! Do you not know? I fear you do not, or you would live differently; do you not know that if you are not entirely reprobate, *Jesus Christ is in you?* Even as the text of last night, the words teach us that the great truth that will lift a Christian out of sin and sloth is the promise of God's indwelling, the consciousness that Jesus Christ is in us.

Know ye not your own selves? Every Christian needs to know himself. Not only his own sinfulness and helplessness, but much more, the divine miracle that has taken place within him and made him the temple and dwelling of the Three-One God. Do learn above everything to know your own selves, that Jesus Christ is in you. There are in every Christian community numbers who are living a low and feeble life, without joy or power over sin, or influence to bless others. To all such the message of St. Paul comes; pause and listen, and take in the wondrous thought, that will be to you both the motive and the power to an entirely new life: *Christ is in you.* If you but learn to believe this, and to give way to it, and to yield yourself to Him, He will do His mighty saving work in you.

You see how we here get at once to the two great questions that occupy us at a Convention like this. The one is, How is it that so many

Christians fail? To this the answer comes: They do not know aright that Jesus Christ is in them. Not one of us could live a worldly life, could give way to pride and selfishness and temper, could so grieve the Holy Spirit of God, if he knew, indeed, that Jesus Christ was in him. The effect of this knowledge would be simply wonderful. On the one hand, it would solemnise and humble, and draw a man to say: I cannot bear the thought of grieving the Christ within me. On the other hand, it would encourage and strengthen him to say: Praise God I have Jesus Christ within me, He will live my life for me. May God bring us to the confession of how much we have lost because we lacked this faith, and teach us to pray much that from moment to moment our life may be: Jesus Christ is in us.

Then comes the other question. If I find that I have not known and lived this life, am I ready to say tonight: Henceforth, by the grace of God, I will. I can rest content with nothing less than the full experience, Jesus Christ is in me? Let us but come in deep poverty and emptiness: He who did the work for us so perfectly on Calvary undertakes to do it in our hearts too. May God by the Holy Spirit, reveal to each of us all that He means us to enjoy. I noticed in our meeting this afternoon many young people: I want to speak as simply as possible, so as to help the very youngest Christian to some right apprehension of this blessed life God has prepared for us. I want to answer some of the questions that may have suggested themselves last night to those to whom this indwelling of God appears something too high and strange. Let us listen in the faith that God Himself will teach us.

Let me say, in the first place, if you would know the power of this life: *Believe in and accept the indwelling Christ.* Let me ask you the question: Do you fully and truly believe in the indwelling Christ? You do believe in an incarnate Christ. When the name of Christ is mentioned, you at once think of One who was born a little babe at Bethlehem, who took our nature upon Him and lived as a man upon earth. That thought is inseparable from your faith in Him. You believe, too, in the crucified Christ, dying on Calvary for our sins. You believe, too, in the risen Saviour, one who lives for evermore. And you believe in the glorified Lord, now sitting on the throne of heaven. But do you believe as definitely—as naturally—in the indwelling Christ? Have you made that one of the articles of your faith, as really as you believe in Christ incarnate or Christ crucified? It is only as this truth is accepted and held that the others can really profit. The experience of the love and the saving power of our incarnate, crucified, glorified Lord depends entirely upon His indwelling in us to reveal His presence and to do His work. If you find your life feeble or sickly, you may be assured that it is because you do not know that Jesus Christ is in you. Do come tonight and begin at once to say: I want with my whole heart to get possessed of this wonderful knowledge, not as a doctrine, but as an experience; Jesus Christ is in me. Begin to believe it at once. Accept of Him, even now, as an indwelling Saviour. Day by day be content with nothing less than the blessed consciousness of His indwelling presence. He loves to reveal Himself.

    I said last night, speaking of God's indwelling, that a man always, to some extent, makes his home the expression of his tastes and character. Even so the Lord Jesus brings the heart which accepts and trusts Him to dwell within, into sympathy and harmony with Himself. And if you ask what the influence is He will exert, the answer is not difficult: He becomes your life, He will live in you, and all that is implied in that wonderful word life, all your thoughts and tempers and dispositions and actions, will have His life and spirit breathing in them. Oh, Christians who have never yet known yourselves that Jesus Christ is in you, believe in Him, accept Him even now as the indwelling Christ.

A second thought: When you accept Christ to dwell in you, be sure and *accept the whole Christ.* There are some people who long for the indwelling Christ, but think of Him chiefly as one who comes to comfort and make glad, to bring peace and joy, but who do not accept of him in all his characters and offices. Beware of being content with only half a Christ; see to it that you have the whole Christ. There are people who accept of Christ as a priest to atone for their sins, but do not yield to His rule as a king; they never think of giving up their own will wholly and entirely to Him. They come to Christ for happiness but not for holiness. They trust in the work He has done for them; they do not surrender themselves to Him for the work He is to do in them. They speak of the forgiveness of sins, but of the cleansing from all unrighteousness they know little. They have not accepted a whole Christ, the Saviour from the power as much as from the guilt of sin.

Let me urge you to make a study of this. As you read of the life of Christ on earth, take every trait of that holy character, as the will of God concerning you. Study His holy humility and meekness, and say, this is the Christ who dwells in me. Look upon His deep dependence upon the Father, and the perfect surrender of His will to do only what pleased the Father, and say, I have yielded myself that my indwelling Lord may work this in me too. As you gaze upon Him as the crucified One, think not only of the Cross in its atonement, as the means of propitiation for your sin, but of its fellowship, as the means of victory over sin. Beware of only saying, Christ crucified *for me,* ever; say too, I am crucified *with Christ.* The one thing for which He lives in you is to breathe His own likeness into your nature, to impart to you His own crucifixion spirit, that blessed disposition that made His sacrifice so well pleasing to the Father. Do accept the whole Christ as dwelling in you.

Especially, do not forget that the Christ who is in you is the loving One, the Servant and the Saviour of the lost. This is the chief mark and glory of the Son of God: that He lived and died, not for Himself, but for others. When He comes to dwell in you, He cannot change His nature; it is the crucified, redeeming Love of God has taken possession of you. Yield yourself to Him that He may breathe into you His own love for souls, His own willingness to give up all, that they maybe saved, His own faith in God's almighty conquering grace. Do accept a whole Christ, a Saviour from all sin and selfishness, a Saviour, not only for yourself, but for all around you.

My third thought. If you accept the whole Christ *accept Him with the whole heart.* Nothing less than this can satisfy God, can secure Christ's full indwelling, can give our heart rest. This was what even the Old Testament demanded: "Thou shalt love the Lord thy God *with all thy heart* and with all thy strength." To it alone the promise was given, Blessed are they which seek Him with *their whole heart.* The old saints made confession: I have sought Thee with *my whole heart.* How can we think that this wondrous New Testament blessing, Jesus Christ, the whole Christ, in us, can be known in power, unless the whole heart be given Him.

With the whole heart—what does that mean? First of all, the heart means love and affection. Our relationship to Christ must not only be that of trust in His help and devotion to His service, but one of intense personal attachment. His heart toward us is all love; His work was and is nothing but the revelation of infinite love and tenderness; and nothing but love on our part can be the proof that we have really accepted and known His love. When Peter had denied Christ, his restoration to Christ's favour and to his place as the shepherd of Christ's flock, all hinged on his answer to the thrice-repeated question, Lovest thou Me? Do not let us think that it is only for women and children, or for mystics and saints, to speak the language of tender, fervent love to the Saviour. If we accept him with the whole heart, let us cultivate an intense personal love. Let us not hesitate to say often, Thou knowest that I love Thee. The heart means love, and the whole heart means love with all our strength.

Then the heart also means the will. Accept Christ with the whole heart—that is to say, give up your will entirely and absolutely to Him. Say to yourself that it is a settled thing that never in anything are you to seek your own will. In things great and small, in decisions of supreme importance, in the most apparently insignificant questions of daily life, live as one who only exists that the will of God and of Christ may be carried out in him. It was to do God's will that Christ came from heaven It is to do God's will in you that he has entered your heart. Beware of hindering or grieving Him in this His blessed work. People sometimes ask: Did not God give us a will for us to use? Is not this man's nobility that he has a will? How can you ask us to give up that will so entirely and absolutely to God? What a misunderstanding the question implies. God gave us a will that with it we might intelligently will what He wills. It is no degradation to a child to give up his will to be guided by that of a wise and loving father. So it is man's highest dignity to find out and accept and delight in the perfect will of God. Accept Christ with the whole heart and a perfect will; count it your true and only blessedness to let Him breathe and work all God's will in you. The whole heart means the whole will given up. Never my own will in anything; let that be the decision with which you bow to let His will rule. And let every sense of difficulty and feebleness only urge you afresh to believe that there is but one way of having your desire fulfilled—accepting Jesus Christ within you as an indwelling Saviour, the living, inspiring power that breathes through all your will. You can have just as much of Christ as you give of yourself to Him: the whole heart can have the whole Christ.

At a meeting of the speakers this afternoon for conversation and prayer, we were asking what is needed to make our Convention a blessing. One said that there seldom was much blessing until there had first come a great breaking down and Christians had been brought to feel how much there is wanting in their life. In England, at Keswick, last year, I heard tell of Conventions where Christians were so convicted of the evil and the shame of their Christian life, that as they left the meeting they hardly dared to speak, and felt driven to go to God and make confession. This is what we need; what we cannot give ourselves; what God can work in us. When once we begin to see that, just as it is a matter of shame and humiliation when a wife has been unfaithful to the husband to whom she had pledged her whole heart, the thought that we have been guilty of withholding from God that undivided love to which, as the allglorious One, our Creator, and our Redeemer, He had such perfect right, ought to bow us in the very dust, then the sense of not having given the whole heart to Christ will become unbearable. As we make confession that we have not given God His glory, that we have sought our own will and honour and pleasure, that we have given self and the world a place in the heart where Christ wanted to dwell alone, God's Holy Spirit can so show us the sinfulness of our Christian life, as to leave us no rest until we have said with full purpose, and the assurance of divine approval: I accept the whole Christ with my whole heart.

Now comes the fourth thought: *Count upon the indwelling Christ to do all in your heart that needs to be done.* In a verse just preceding our text, Paul says: "Ye seek for a proof of Christ speaking in me." It was not only Christ living in him, but Christ acting and speaking through him, they looked for. The Corinthians were justified in that expectation. And so when Christ comes in to take possession, He will by His Spirit do within us what we cannot do. He will make you what God would have you be—conformable to the image of His Son. It is utterly vain for us to think of following Christ's steps, or imitating His example, or copying His life, by any effort of ours. Jesus lived upon earth a human life that he might show us what the life is we are to live. But what folly for us to think now we are Christians, that we can or shall approach to anything like His life. It is impossible. We are, indeed, called to it. It is our first duty. But it can only be if we let Himself live that life in us. The life of Christ is altogether too high and too divine for us to reproduce. It is His own life, and only His. But He will live it out in us. You would fain be humble, or patient, or gentle. How often you have prayed and struggled, but all in vain. You sought for a humility here on earth, in yourself, something like that which He, as God, brought from heaven. What folly. Oh, learn to cease from self and its efforts. Turn inward; let faith be occupied with and rest in the Almighty indwelling One, who has become your life for the very purpose of filling it with His own. Count upon Him who dwells within to do the work He has undertaken. When he was upon earth, He began His life as a little babe, unknown and very feeble. He grew up in seclusion, and no one thought that this was the Redeemer of men. When He began His public ministry He lifted not up his voice in the streets; He was despised and rejected of men; they knew not that He was the Lord of Glory. Even so within thy heart, His appearance will be low and feeble and scarce to be observed. Then comes the time to heed His command: only believe. Trust in Him with an unmeasured confidence, that He will do His work within you in His own way and time. However slow and hidden and all unlikely things seem to be within, hold fast your confidence that He is there, and that He is working, and that in due time He will reveal Himself.

Dear Christians, when you believe in the incarnate or the crucified Christ, it means that you believe that He did the work perfectly, for which He came to live and die upon earth. When you believe in the risen and glorified Lord, it means that you have no shadow of doubt but that He is now living and reigning at God's right hand, in divine power. Let your faith in the indwelling One be as simple and clear. The work for which He entered your heart, the great work of possessing and renewing and glorifying your whole inner life, He will do in wondrous power and love. Trust Him for it; the Christ of Bethlehem, the Christ of Calvary, the Christ of the Throne in heaven, is the Christ in you. Do begin to believe: Jesus Christ is in me; Jesus Christ will do the work perfectly in me. Just listen to that wonderful promise in Hebrews: "The God of peace perfect you in every good work, that ye may do His will, *working in you* that which is pleasing in His sight, through Jesus Christ." *Yes, through Jesus Christ!* If it is through Jesus Christ that God Himself works in you, how can this be in any other way but Jesus Christ Himself being in you? God fits you to do His will through Jesus Christ dwelling in you. Doubt no longer, but rejoice. Know your own selves that Jesus Christ is in you.

More than one is doubtless asking: Can this really be? Oh, that I knew what is needed to have Christ Himself dwelling in me. You find the answer in the simple, well-known words: "My son, give Me thine heart." Have you in very deed done that? I do not ask. Are you believers? Are you sure that your sins are pardoned? Are you seeking to live a Christian life? But have you given your heart to Christ to possess, to rule, to renew, to dwell in all alone, to fill with the will of God? Have you given it away, out of your power into His? Your self-confidence, your self-contentment, your self-pleasing, your self-will, has it all been laid at Christ's feet? so that He can cast it out, and fill the heart with Himself. If not, let nothing keep you back from giving now what belongs to God, and what Christ came to win back for Him. Your heart was made for God. A man has the wondrous power of in one moment setting his heart upon some object that strongly attracts him, or that has won his affection—of giving away his heart. At this moment bow in penitence and shame that you have so little known that Jesus Christ is in you, and have so little, day by day, yielded up the whole being to Him. Bow in lowly confession, and offer Him even now this sin-stained and unworthy heart, and believe that He takes possession. What I give, God takes; what God takes He will hold and keep through Jesus Christ. Blessed Lord! even now we give ourselves, and know Thou dost accept, that Thou art within, and that Thou wilt fill us with Thyself.

4

Daily Fellowship with God.

THE FIRST AND chief need of our Christian life is —*fellowship with God.*

The divine life within us comes from God, and is entirely dependent upon Him. As I need every moment afresh the air to breathe, as the sun every moment afresh sends down its light, so it is only in direct living communication with God that my soul can be strong.

The manna of one day was corrupt when the next day came. I must every day have fresh grace from heaven; and I obtain it only in direct waiting upon God Himself. Begin each day by tarrying before God, and letting Him touch you. Take time to meet God.

To this end let the first act in your devotions be a setting yourself still before God. In prayer or worship everything depends upon God taking the chief place. I must bow quietly before Him in humble faith and adoration. God is. God is near. God is love, longing to communicate Himself to me. God the Almighty One, who worketh all in all, is even now waiting to work in me, and make Himself known.

Take time, till you know God is very near.

When you have given God His place, of honour, glory, and power, take your place of deepest lowliness, and seek to be filled with the spirit of humility. As a creature it is your blessedness to be nothing, that God may be all in you. As a sinner you are not worthy to look up to God; bow in self-abasement. As a saint, let God's love overwhelm you, and bow you still lower down. Sink down before Him in humility, meekness, patience, and surrender to His goodness and mercy. He will exalt you.

Oh, take time, to get very low before God.

Then accept and value your place in Christ Jesus. God delights in nothing but his beloved Son, and can be satisfied with nothing less in those who draw nigh to Him. Enter deep into God's holy presence in the boldness which the blood gives, and in the assurance that in Christ you are most well-pleasing. In Christ you are within the veil. You have access into the very heart and love of the Father. This is the great object of fellowship with God, that I may have more of God in my life, and that God may see Christ formed in me. Be silent before God, and let Him bless you.

This Christ is a living Person. He loves you with a personal love, and He looks every day for the personal response of your love. Look into His face with trust, till His love really shines into your heart. Make His heart glad by telling Him that you do love Him. He offers Himself to you as a personal Saviour and Keeper from the power of sin. Do not ask, Can I be kept from sinning, if I keep close to Him? but ask, Can I be kept from sinning, *if he always keeps close to me?* and you see at once how safe it is to trust Him.

We have not only Christ's life in us as a power, and His presence with us as a person, but we have His likeness to be wrought unto us. He is to be formed in us, so that His form or figure, His image can be seen in us. Bow before God until you get some sense of the greatness and blessedness of the work to be carried on by God in you this day. Say to God, "Father, here am I for Thee to give as much in me of Christ's likeness as I can receive." And wait to hear Him say, "My child, I give thee as much of Christ as thy heart is open to receive." The God who revealed Jesus in the flesh and perfected Him, will reveal Him in thee and perfect thee in Him. The Father loves the Son, and delights to work out His image and likeness in thee. Count upon it that this blessed work will be done in thee as thou waitest on thy God, and holdest fellowship with Him.

The likeness to Christ consists chiefly in two things—the likeness of His death and resurrection (*Romans 6:5*). The death of Christ was the consummation of His humility and obedience, the entire giving up of His life to God. In Him we are dead to sin. As we sink down in humility and dependence and entire surrender to God, the power of His death works in us, and we are made conformable to His death. And so we know Him in the power of His resurrection, in the victory over sin, and all the joy and power of the risen life, Therefore, every morning, "present yourselves unto God as those that are alive from the dead." He will maintain the life He gave, and bestow the grace to live as risen ones.

All this can only be in the power of the Holy Spirit, who dwells in you. Count upon Him to glorify Christ in you. Count upon Christ to increase in you the inflowing of His Spirit. As you wait before God to realise His presence, remember that the Spirit is in you to reveal the things of God. Seek in God's presence to have the anointing of the Spirit of Christ so truly that your whole life may every moment be spiritual.

As you meditate on this wondrous salvation, and seek full fellowship with the great and holy God, and wait on Him to reveal Christ in you you will feel how needful is the giving up of all to receive Him. Seek grace, to know what it means to live as wholly for God as Jesus did. Only the Holy Spirit Himself can teach you what an entire yielding of the whole life to God can mean. Wait on God to show you in this what you do not know. Let every approach to God, and every request for fellowship with Him, be accompanied by a new, very definite, and entire surrender to Him to work in you.

"By faith." Here, as through all Scripture and all the spiritual life this must be the keynote. As you tarry before God, let it be in a deep, quiet faith in Him, the Invisible One, who is so near, so holy, so mighty, so loving. In a deep, restful faith, too, that all the blessings and powers of the heavenly life are around you, and in you. Just yield yourself in the faith of a perfect trust to the ever-blessed Holy Trinity, to work out all God's purpose in you. Begin each day thus in fellowship with God, and God will be all in all to you.

Manufactured by Amazon.ca
Bolton, ON